CUP WINNERS

Martin Waddell

Illustrated by David Price

Inflatable F.A. Cup!

OXFORD
UNIVERSITY PRESS

Great Clarendon Street, Oxford OX2 6DP

Oxford University Press is a department of the University of Oxford.
It furthers the University's objective of excellence in research, scholarship,
and education by publishing worldwide in

Oxford   New York

Auckland   Cape Town   Dar es Salaam   Hong Kong   Karachi
Kuala Lumpur   Madrid   Melbourne   Mexico City   Nairobi
New Delhi   Shanghai   Taipei   Toronto

With offices in

Argentina   Austria   Brazil   Chile   Czech Republic   France   Greece
Guatemala   Hungary   Italy   Japan   Poland   Portugal   Singapore
South Korea   Switzerland   Thailand   Turkey   Ukraine   Vietnam

Oxford is a registered trade mark of Oxford University Press
in the UK and in certain other countries

British Library Cataloguing in Publication Data

Data available

ISBN: 978-0-19-919630-2

9 10 8

Mixed Pack (1 of 6 different titles): ISBN: 978-0-19-919632-6
Class Pack (6 copies of 6 titles): ISBN: 978-0-19-919631-9

Illustrated by David Price c/o J Martin & Artists
Cover illustration by Martin McKenna

Paper used in the production of this book is a natural,
recyclable product made from wood grown in sustainable forests.
The manufacturing process conforms to the environmental
regulations of the country of origin.

Acknowledgements
p 1 Ben Radford/Allsport (UK) Ltd.; p 4 (left) Allsport (UK) Ltd.;
p 4 (centre) Press Association; p 4 (right) Andrew Cowie/
Colorsport; pp 4/5 Corel; p 5 (top left) Ben Radford/Allsport (UK)
Ltd.; p 5 (top right) Action Images; p 5 (bottom right) Colorsport;
p 7 Press Association; p 10 Science Photo Library; p 14 Rex
Features; p 16 Action Images; p 17 Andrew Cowie/Colorsport;
pp 20/21 Andrew Cowie/Colorsport; p 22 Colorsport; p 25
Colorsport; pp 28/29 Allsport (UK) Ltd.; p 31 Colorsport; p 32
Colorsport; p 34 Colorsport; p 36 Andrew Cowie/Colorsport;
p 38 Allsport (UK) Ltd.; p 42 Allsport (UK) Ltd.; pp 46/47 Corel;
p 47 Martin Waddell

Printed in China by Imago

Contents

Introduction

No two Cup Finals are ever the same.
Each has its stars, and its story.

These stories come from F.A. Cup
Finals played in the last
50 years.

Look through this book
to find the Finals that are
shown here.

What is special about
the F.A. Cup shown here?

One man can change the course of a game.

Stan Matthews did it for Blackpool, playing against Bolton Wanderers in 1953. The game has gone down in history as "The Matthews' Final," although another Blackpool and England player, Stan Mortenson, scored a hat-trick.

Blackpool were trailing with twenty minutes left. Mortenson had scored his first goal, but Blackpool were losing 1–3. Subs were not allowed in those days and Bolton had two injured players... but they held on to their lead grimly.

Then Stan Matthews took over. The England ace tore at the Bolton defence again and again. He turned the defenders inside out, with the crowd roaring him on.

A cross to Stan Mortenson... and Mortenson scored his second goal of the match.

Mortenson scores the second goal

Blackpool won a free kick outside the box. Mortenson took it... and scored again, completing his hat-trick. The score was 3–3.

Extra time looked certain.

Then Matthews took off on another run. He beat two men, and carried the ball to the touchline. He played an accurate cut-back to Bill Perry... and Perry crashed the ball home.

The stadium erupted!

Blackpool had won the Cup!

Result: Blackpool 4 : Bolton Wanderers 3.

It was Stan's day... both of the Stans.

CHAPTER 2

Bert Trautmann was a great keeper. But what makes him stand out in the history of the F.A. Cup happened with fifteen minutes to go in the final.

Manchester were winning 3–1.

Birmingham's Peter Murphy lunged for the ball, as Trautmann dropped on it. Save... but the goalkeeper lay still on the turf.

Trautmann got to his feet and played on, dazed and distracted. He had to. Subs weren't allowed then.

Manchester guarded him as best they could. They held out until the final whistle.

Three days later, X-rays showed that Trautmann had played through the last fifteen minutes of the game with a broken neck!

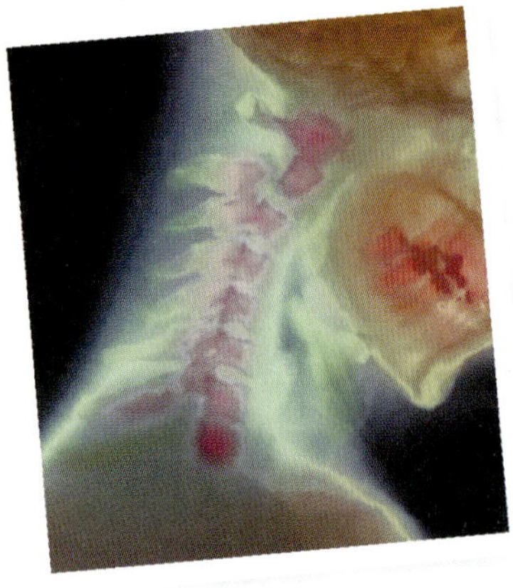

X-ray showing a broken neck

Result: Birmingham City 1 : Manchester City 3.

Trautmann could have died for his team... and the Cup!

They don't come much better than the Liverpool team who played in this Final. England's Peter Beardsley was the link man. Ireland's John Aldridge was the high-scoring striker. Big game players included Bruce Grobbelaar, Alan Hansen and John Barnes.

The "Pool" had won the League by a nine point margin.

Wimbledon had risen from the old Southern League to the top Division in eleven years. The so-called "Crazy Gang" were long-ball no-hopers.

Liverpool only had to turn up to win the Cup. The only question was how much they would win by.

They reckoned without Wimbledon goalkeeper, Dave Beasant.

Liverpool attacked, and Beasant saved again and again.

Then Lawrie Sanchez nodded a cross from Dennis Wise past Bruce Grobbelaar to put the Dons in front, 1–0.

The Crazy Gang couldn't win it... could they?

Liverpool came out for the second half determined to attack.

Dave saved brilliantly from Houghton, and then from Hansen.

Then Liverpool were awarded a penalty. Aldridge stepped up to take it.

No striker had ever missed from the spot in a Wembley Final.

No keeper had ever saved a spot kick.

It was big Dave's moment.

Aldridge, goal-scoring ace, hit the ball... Dave dived... SAVE!

Dave Beasant saves the day!

Result: Liverpool 0 : Wimbledon 1.

Wimbledon took the Cup... and it was their Captain, Dave Beasant, who climbed the Wembley steps to accept it.

England star Paul Gascoigne (Gazza) had shone in Spurs' 3-1 semi-final victory over North London rivals Arsenal. The power of Gazza's free kick goal, scored after only five minutes of play, had overshadowed his team-mate Gary Lineker's two goals.

Gazza was about to make a big-money move to Italy. And Spurs fans were counting on a brilliant game from their departing hero.

The game began. Gascoigne set off like a misguided missile. He was running everywhere, lunging and tackling.

With only fifteen minutes gone, an out-of-control Gazza crash-tackled the Forest full back, Gary Charles.

The tackle could have ended Charles' playing career... Luckily, it didn't.

Gazza tackling
Gary Charles

Paul Gascoigne lies injured

It was Gascoigne who had to leave the field on a stretcher, his knee badly injured. The injury probably saved him from getting a red card for dangerous play.

Nottingham's Stuart Pearce crashed the ball home from the free kick which resulted.

Spurs fought back, without their star player. They equalized.

It was 1–1 at full time.

But an own goal by Forest's Des Walker won the game for Spurs.

Result: Tottenham Hotspur 2 : Nottingham Forest 1.

It was Tottenham's Cup… no thanks to their "star".

Manchester were a team of stars, but two players stood out from the others. They were the young David Beckham and the experienced Eric (Ooh-Ah!) Cantona.

Cantona had missed the 1995 Final when United lost 1-0 to Everton. Now he had another chance. Becks was already a household name.

Alex Ferguson's team had just overcome a nine point disadvantage in the league to win the Premiership title.

Now, only a Liverpool line-up that included James, Fowler, Collymore, Barnes and McManaman stood between United and winning the Cup and League double.

CHAPTER 5

It was a close, hard-fought struggle. Becks got on the end of Ryan Giggs' through ball. He hit a rocket shot... but keeper David James saved it.

Cantona fed Andy Cole... who missed! Five minutes left, and still no score.

Becks took a corner.

Liverpool keeper David James

A poor clearance from Liverpool and twenty metres out, the ball fell to Ooh-Ah!

Cantona's shot rippled the net. The game was over.

Manchester United 1 : Liverpool 0.

A winner's medal for Beckham... but it was Ooh-Ah's day!

Ooh-Ah does it again!

Great managers don't score goals, but they play a huge part in moulding any successful team.

Bill Shankly of Liverpool and Don Revie of Leeds each put their stamp on their teams. Liverpool and Leeds went on to dominate English football for a long time.

This was a match studded with stars.

For Shankly's Reds: Lawrence, Yeats, Callaghan, Hunt, St. John.

For Don Revie's United: Sprake, Hunter, Jackie Charlton, Bremner, Giles, Collins.

Great managers, great players... but it was a tense, difficult game, with both teams fighting hard. The score was 0–0 after ninety minutes.

All the goals came in extra time, as the two teams tired.

Hunt scored for Liverpool and Bremner put it in the net for Leeds.

The score was 1–1.

CHAPTER 6

The game was won when Liverpool's Ian St. John met Callaghan's cross with a flying header. The ball flew past Gary Sprake in the Leeds goal.

Ian St. John scores the winning goal

Result: Liverpool 2 : Leeds United 1.

The clash between the two great managers ended in a win for Shankly and Liverpool.

Don Revie had to wait another seven years to win the F.A. Cup for Leeds.

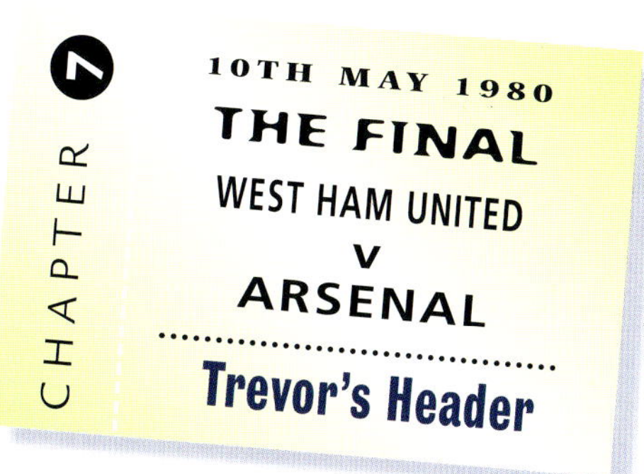

Trevor Brooking of West Ham was an elegant, strolling figure on the pitch at Upton Park.

He could change the course of a game with a telling pass, or powerful shot at goal but...

...Trevor didn't head many goals.

In a long career for the Hammers and England, Trevor had scored only three goals using his head.

So who's not going to score a winning Cup Final goal with a header?

That's what everyone thought... except, maybe, Trevor in his dreams.

But that's just what happened.

The West Ham winner didn't come from one of the stylish moves for

which the Hammers were famous.

Striker Stuart Pearson shot for goal, and miss-hit his shot.

Who got on the end of it?

It was Trevor Brooking.

The ball sped into the back of the net off Brooking's head, past an astonished Pat Jennings.

Trevor Brooking scores the winner for West Ham

That was it. Trevor's header... the winning goal!

Result: West Ham 1 : Arsenal 0.

It was a goal that surprised everyone... even Trevor!

14TH MAY 1991
The Final
Replay
TOTTENHAM HOTSPUR
v
MANCHESTER CITY

RICKY'S REPLAY

Ricky Villa celebrates with the F.A. Cup Trophy

The hundredth Cup Final... and there were two of them.

The first game, had ended 1–1. Tommy Hutchison scored for City, and then scored an own-goal to equalize for Spurs.

Glen Hoddle
and Ossie
Ardiles

Another player got on the score sheet twice in the replay.

This time it was Tottenham's Ricky Villa. He played badly in the first game, and had been substituted. So Ricky, who was a World Cup winner for Argentina, had something to prove in the replay.

The Tottenham team was built round the skills of Ossie Ardiles and the playmaking of Glenn Hoddle.

They soon went in front... and it was Ricky who scored.

1–0 for Spurs.

But the match wasn't over yet.

City fought back to 2–2.

Then came Ricky's winner... the wonder goal by which this Final will always be remembered.

A thirty-metre, turning, twisting run took Ricky past three defenders... just for good value, he beat one of them twice... and into the box.

Joe Corrigan raced out from the City goal.

Ricky's carefully placed shot hit the back of the net.

Result: Tottenham Hotspur 3 : Manchester City 2.

The stadium rose to cheer Ricky.

Ricky scores the winning goal for Tottenham

12TH MAY 1979
THE FINAL
ARSENAL
v
MANCHESTER UNITED

BRADY'S GAME

Liam Brady played many times for
Arsenal and the Republic of Ireland.

This was his Cup Final, although a
brilliant United fight back almost cost
the Gunners the Cup.

Brady was everywhere, passing, sprinting, dribbling. He was a big star on the big stage, about to collect his winner's medal.

Five minutes to go, and Arsenal were 2–0 up. The game was in their grasp, but...

Gordon McQueen, the Manchester player, came through and scored.

Still 2–1 to Arsenal.

Just over three minutes to go...

...Sammy McIlroy grabbed an equalizer for United.

That made it 2–2.

Sammy McIlroy scores United's second goal

The last minute of the game. Extra time loomed.

Liam saw his chance slipping away, but he didn't give in. The weaving, jinking Irishman tore into the heart of the United defence with the ball at his feet.

Graham Rix got clear with the ball. He centred, and his cross was met by Alan Sunderland, who slid the ball into the Manchester net.

Alan Sunderland's goal won the game, but Liam Brady had stamped his name on the game.

Result: Manchester United 2 : Arsenal 3.

The ball hit the net with only fifty seconds remaining of the ninety minutes.

Alan Sunderland celebrates his goal against Man. Utd

Liverpool and Arsenal again... but this time in Cardiff's Millennium Stadium.

It was a great stage, for a great player. They don't come much greater than Michael Owen. Robbie Fowler was on the bench... and many people felt he should have been in the team. It was up to Owen to justify his manager's selection.

On a searing hot day, Fredrik Ljunberg put Arsenal in front in the 72nd minute.

Liverpool brought on Fowler and Berger, in an attempt to turn things round. Robbie and Michael... could one of them save the game?

Still 1-0 to Arsenal, and only seven minutes left. Liverpool's Babbel headed on McAllister's free kick.

It was Michael who crashed the ball home. 1–1.

Liverpool saw hope... but the clock was against them.

Six minutes to go, five, four, three, two... and Patrick Berger played a long ball.

Michael Owen again!

He sped past Arsenal's Lee Dixon and shot...

GOAL!

Michael Owen scoring the winner against Arsenal

Result: Arsenal 1 : Liverpool 2.

Michael Owen enjoyed his day-out in Wales!

Ian Wright first came to fame at Crystal Palace, in a goal-scoring partnership with Mark Bright.

Then, in the 1989–90 season, he broke his leg.

Crystal Palace reached the Cup Final, but their ace striker Wright wasn't really fit enough to play. He had a pain-killing injection, and Palace put him on the bench. They thought they might need him.

And they did.

United went 2–1 up in the 62nd minute, when Mark Hughes scored.

Palace were on their way out... Then on came Ian.

Just ten minutes later, he had scored. 2–2. Level pegging.

The game went to extra time.

Two minutes gone, and Wright volleyed Palace back in front!

2–3 to Palace.

It looked as though Ian had proved himself the (W)right man, but...

Mark Hughes grabbed a late equalizer for United... And they won the replay as well.

It happens. Even winning stars don't always win.

Result: Manchester United 3 : Crystal Palace 3.

Replay 17th May 2001 : Manchester United 1 : Crystal Palace 0.

The Wright man lost that day. But he went on to become a footballing legend with the Gunners, and England.

Dream Team

This is a Dream Team picked from the players mentioned in this book:

Could they come together to make a team?
Pick your Dream Team to beat them!

I was almost
a professional
footballer once, but
I didn't quite make it.

Martin Waddell as a young footballer

It is very important
to write about things
that really interest you.
If a writer is interested
in what he or she writes about, it
bursts through onto the page. If the
writer is bored, the reader will be too.

Lesson one in being a writer: If you
want to write well, chose something
that matters to you. Never write about
things you find boring!

Martin Waddell

Index

Players and Managers